THE ROAD TO
TAPPAHANNOCK
and Other Poems

THE ROAD TO TAPPAHANNOCK
and Other Poems

E. M. Adams

authorHOUSE®

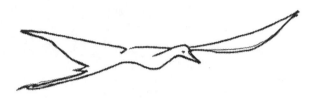

<u>*Dedication*</u>

To my Husband and to my Father, both men of letters,
for their insight and support over the years.
And to my Mother,
who loved poetry and the written word,
who was at heart, a poet.

AuthorHouse™
1663 Liberty Drive
Bloomington, IN 47403
www.authorhouse.com
Phone: 1-800-839-8640

Published by AuthorHouse   03/04/2013

ISBN: 978-1-4817-0841-8 (sc)
ISBN: 978-1-4817-0839-5 (hc)
ISBN: 978-1-4817-0840-1 (e)

Library of Congress Control Number: 2013901071

This book is printed on acid-free paper.

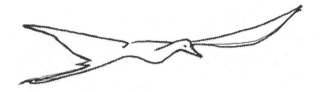

The Road To Tappahannock
And Other Poems

Contents

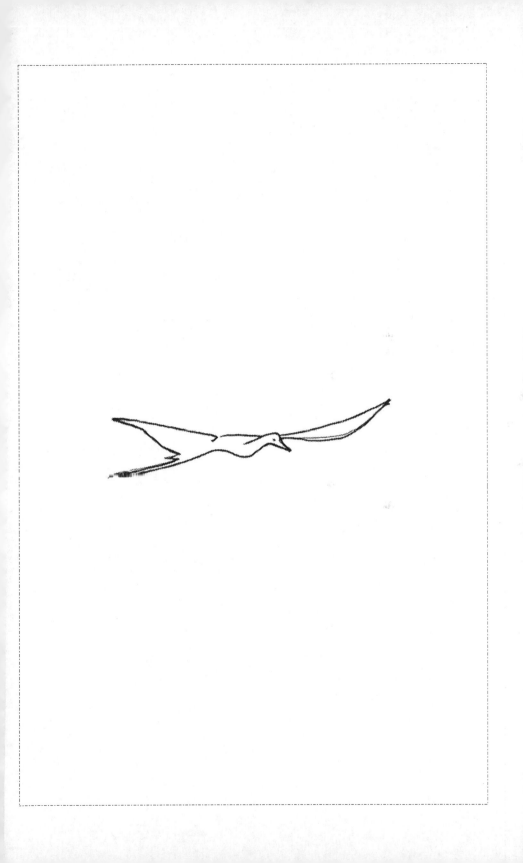

THE ROAD TO TAPPAHANNOCK

And Other Poems

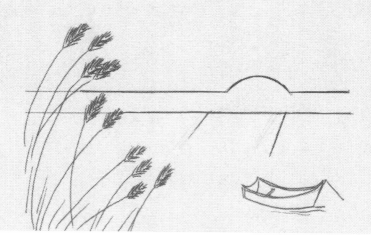

THE ROAD TO TAPPAHANNOCK

In the state of Virginia, there is an exquisitely forested and beautiful strip of road on Rt. 17 just south of Massaponox. The trees are quite tall and their tops meet high above the center of the road. As you ride along, you feel you are moving through the center of a great cathedral. If you travel the road often, you see the changes for every season. The trees and the road never twice appear the same.

The poem "The Road to Tappahannock" describes the lovely changes that can be seen every season of the year when traveling this wonderful, scenic road.

The Road to Tappahannock

The White Cathedral

Silent and glowing, white as
Pearl in winter snow,
The winding road goes gracefully along,
Showing tall and arching winter limbs
Of trees bare and gray
That give no glimpse of
Hovering winter skies above.
Seemingly cold, but warm with snow light.

The Spring Cathedral

And now in April, always a surprise,
Though known and not unexpected,
Those same tall and arching trees are
Many shades of color green
From lime to auburn jade.
Added to the gift are drifts of
Dogwood and purple redbud trees
Whose color bounces gaily off
A sometimes shot of impossibly blue skies.

The Green Cathedral

Arching overhead and covered in
High summer's greenest greens,
The tall and graceful silent trees
Appear like green hands
Uplifted towards the sun,
Kindly shading what's beneath
With gentle joy.
The trip along the graceful,
Winding road
Through softened sunlit, glittering,
Cool, and fluttering leaves,
Is all too short.
The green cathedral sighs
An invitation to return.

The Gold Cathedral

And now, in arching trees above,
The leaves are every color bright
From russet to yellow to orange to lime
Turned by sunlight into
Shades of priceless gold,
Laced with multicolored
Shades of green and blue.
Reminders of soaring stone cathedral walls
With windows of colored, leaded glass,
Shining in the sun.

The "Come Here"

The history of the area around the Northern Neck and Tappahannock, Virginia, can be traced back to the original settlers of the United States. The native Indian peoples lived here ahead of the settlers. The land had been occupied for many years. If you are a longtime resident, you know everyone within a hundred miles.

Therefore, if you are new to the area, you are gently known, for a while, as a

"Come Here."

The "Come Here"

If I were a Tappahannock native,
I might not love it so.
I would think the quiet and the
Solitude was usual.
The cooling breeze and sweet
Twittering songs of birds
Would be so common as to be,
For a Tappahannock native,
An invisible occurrence.
And nature's slow recurrence
From one season to the next,
Mixing sun and shade,
Wind and rain with fragrant spring
And summer blooms, would be,
For the Tappahannock native,
Like breathing.
But if so fortunate as to be a "Come Here,"
All those things and more,
Are new and crystal clear.
So wonderful to contemplate
While watching the "Rivah"
Flowing slowly by.

A Poem a Day
and
Silent Moment in Tappahannock

were written during days of wonderful summer weather in
Tappahannock when it was quiet, cool and breezy.
There was time to be alone, to enjoy the porch, the weather, and
the surrounding marshy river scene.

<u>A Poem a Day</u>

Here in Tappahannock,
Sitting on the porch,
Amidst quiet of brooding trees
And sun and cool and warm and hot,
Watching roses bloom and flowers grow
And marsh turn green in summer heat,
And birds of every colored feather
Beat wings and fly about.
The muse inspires a poem every day.

<u>Silent Moment in Tappahannock</u>

Sweet morning breeze across the Rappahannock,
Breakfast on the screened-in porch,
Whispering leaves of oak:
Silence.
Songbirds, bluebirds, eagles, and coral-colored roses,
Fluffy clouds, the promise of rain,
Dragonflies:
More silence.
Twitters and tweets of many different birds,
Pleasant musical accompaniment for nature's:
Silence

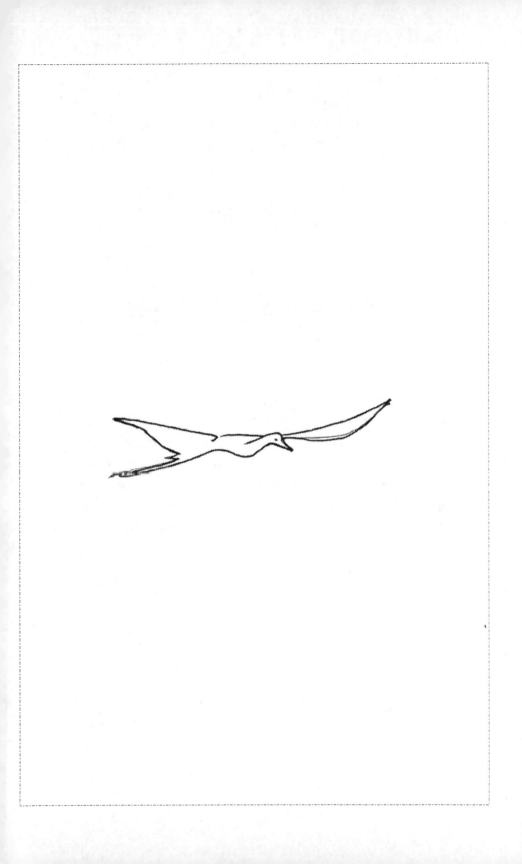

<u>A Hidden Shady Corner</u>

The Rappahannock River in Virginia is a haven for the bald eagle. Their population has expanded a great deal in the last few years. It is often possible to detect them all along the river, and no matter how often they are observed, they are always a treat to see. Eagles can sometimes be seen up close, but most times one sees them at a distance in the sky over the river when they are fishing for dinner.

A Hidden Shady Corner

In a hidden shady corner on the deck,
Alone in quiet, dark and breezy, cool,
White roses bloom fluorescent in the sun,
Bright and silent against
Green grass and green marsh,
Where sleep and napping is the rule.
Over the river blue and gleaming,
Hunting eagles fly, quickly lost
To eyesight in the pale and
Cloudy sky,
Silent and perfect in
The blue and green and wide.

A Wish for Nature

Some time ago, for a period Tappahannock's quiet nearby towns and areas began to grow at what seemed to be a very rapid pace. One of the nicest things about the area is its quiet and its open, country feel.

Several lots in the area are ready to accept new homes. So at one point not long ago, it seemed as if there might be a lot of building going on and more people moving in.

There are laws that protect the wetlands, but one can only hope the laws will protect the most wild and beautiful sights along the river.

A Wish for Nature

If I could save this day,
If I could save this day so fine,
If I could save the air,
If I could only save this lovely breeze,
And save this miracle day
That swells so softly all around,
Unselfconscious and unassuming.

It is my hope that this wild-treed scene
Will last as long as ages past,
That no man comes with axes and
Machines
To strip the river's edge of green,
Of bright and foggy, misty scenes,
Of wild creatures' homes serene,
Of eloquent quiet and nature's dream,
Of herons, ospreys or eagle's scream.

A Trace of Summer on the Wind, Arriving Rain and Storm Upon the River

are poems written separately but tell the story of weather
experiences possible along the "Rivah."

<u>A Trace of Summer on the Wind</u>

Breeze across the river does it come,
Cooling with an icy bite.
So welcome in the summer sun.
The smell of briny marsh
At lowering of tide it brings.
It kisses me with icy kiss,
It brings the call of heron harsh.
Is it more than one could wish?

Arriving Rain

Rain, it comes from a long way off;
It comes from the north and from
The farthest ocean.
Rain comes across the mountains and
Across the plains
Then across the mountains once
Again
To here.
But it is not yet here.
It comes first midst fluffy clouds and
Sun.
It comes on exquisite soft and
Sunny breeze
That becomes light wind.
Then all is warm and still.
The air turns dense and clouds hang
Low
And so they seem to touch the trees,
And then, of course, you wait,
Until the rain arrives.

Storm Upon the River

A flash of lightning in the west,
Black clouds billow darkly in the sky.
The wind, too, dark and swift
And wild and strong, brings
With it the slashing rain.
It blows the trees and fiercely waves
About their branches and their leaves.
It makes a loud and frightening noise.
But, oh, how exciting
Is the scene to make you feel
Wild as wind and rain.
Quick, close the windows;
Rush inside,
Watch the storm and lightning
From behind the windowpane.

In Tappahannock, along the Rappahannock River, with the tidal and low water there exist marshes with tall grasses that harbor all sorts of wildlife.
It is wonderful to watch the marsh in all weather and all seasons. The ospreys, herons, eagles, bluebirds, turtles, foxes, and so many other wild things are delightful to see.
These were the inspiration for the following three poems:

<u>A Poem on My Mind</u>

<u>The Marsh,</u>

and

<u>Blue Heron</u>

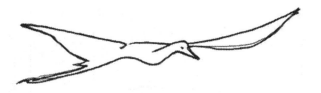

A Poem on My Mind

I feel a poem coming on,
A window for your world.
My eyes look on the world
And mostly does such beauty see:
The trees, the marsh, the river
In every season new and shining,
Blooms beautiful and bright,
With every season's colors changing.
Even though in all years nature is the same,
It seems surprising to the eyes
And different every time,
So ideas new arise.
For your pleasure, nature's colors
Change every season in a slow,
But inexorable, plan.
Together can we share the beauty that we see.
From my eyes a poem of nature
As a window for your world will be.

<u>The Marsh</u>

In summer the marsh grass stands
Lush and green and ochre
With waving tips of burnished bronze.
From a distance, still and silent it appears,
But a closer look reveals its muddy home
For snakes and fish and birds and
Bugs and all animal life diverse.
In fall the marsh grass grows dry
To change into an autumn gold
As weather goes from warm to cold.
And then the marsh grass turns
To beige and brown to hibernate
Until the warm spring comes around.
So the cycle starts anew,
Anticipated with excitement as before,
When warm rain and weather
Slowly turn again the marsh
To beautiful, lush, and silky green.

<u>Blue Heron</u>

Squawk! Squawk! There he is.
He gives himself away:
Sailing, big and blue and wide,
Disappearing with slow grace into
Green, yellow, and ochre marsh.
There he remains unseen until
Another squawk is heard and
He again appears to fly
On giant wings away.
At times he flies to nearby woods
Perching impossibly, it seems,
On one tree's outer limb.
Or topping the marsh,
Just above the grass, he glides
Silently and gracefully along,
On narrow, long, blue wings.
Over the shining river.

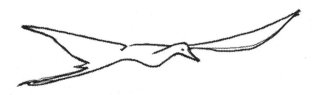

A ride along the James and York Rivers near
Williamsburg, Virginia, in late afternoon just before
sunset will treat the observer to a scene of blue and gold
delight: of gold marsh grass and vivid blue sky.
These were the inspiration for the poem.

Tidewater Girl

<u>*Tidewater Girl*</u>

A pretty girl is the Tidewater Girl
So soft and sweet and smiling,
Soft as a summer Tidewater breeze
And sweet as the smell of boxwood.
Eyes a copy of blue Tidewater skies,
Hair gold like the golden Tidewater marsh.
Her eyes twinkle as they meet with her smile
Along with a melodious greeting.
So what is the harm of being disarmed?
Just smile, and succumb to the charm
Of the beautiful Tidewater Girl.

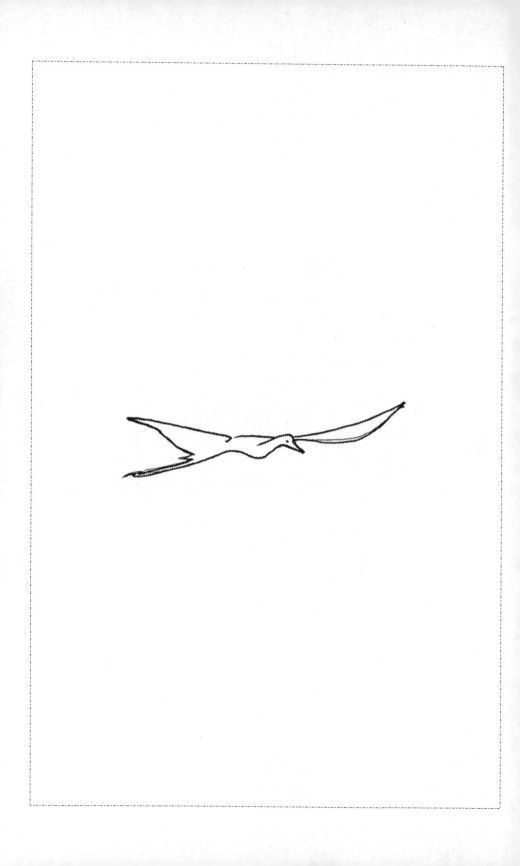

BEACHES, BOATS AND SHIPS

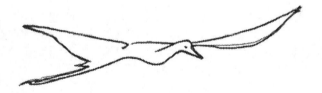

The Dolphin and the Magic Mermaid

This poem was written in Destin, Florida, after I came upon a fantastic, lifelike sand sculpture of a mermaid and a dolphin on the beach. Sadly, of course, it was not permanent and would be washed out to sea with the tide.

The Dolphin and the Magic Mermaid

Sun and sand and light and sound,
Sun and sea and ocean's pound,
All in sun-kissed light is found,
All in a shining ball is bound.
In the turquoise ocean bright
The Magic Mermaid and Dolphin swim.
The pale gray Dolphin glides and grins,
To break the water's surface now and
Then to show his shining fin.
The Mermaid hums and sings
A watery mermaid song
Swirling her scaly tail with
Ever a radiant smile.
Within the waves her golden
Seaweed hair streams bright.
The Dolphin and The Mermaid say,
It's time to take a rest
They see a pure white sandy beach
On which to make a nest.
Using magic powers they possess
They land upon the shore
To hide disguised as sculptures in the sand.
The Mermaid uses shells for scales and
Small beach stones for clothes.
Seaweed and sand create
Her golden hair of waves.
A black shell makes up the
Plump and smiling dolphin's eye.
Passing humans, unaware it is not real,
Admire the magic scene
And speak about its charm.
At turn of tide, the waves come in
To break the magic spell.
They wash the Dolphin and the
Magic Mermaid out to sea again.

Beach Scene

Spring Break in Destin, Florida, is a very happy and exciting time for the college students who come to the beach. This year the students had a marvelous time. Even though a lot of beer was consumed, and there was much singing and hanging out, they were very well behaved, energetic, and beautiful young people. The poem was written while enjoying the beach scene from the balcony.

Beach Scene

Bronze goddesses in fluorescent pink bikinis
Walk the beach with strong,
Confident and joyful strides.
Young revelers mass near the waves
To sing and dance and party.
Dark silhouettes swim in crystal waters in
Shades of turquoise and minty blue,
Iced with white and frothy foam.
Here comes the ice cream truck
playing "La Cucaracha" or
"Way Down upon the Suwannee River."
And in the middle of the bright and shining sea
Sails, a Hobie Cat as fast as can be, Flying
Fluorescent orange, brown, and yellow, stripes.
See the beach umbrellas of blue and purple and
Bright multicolor, to match the towels upon the sand.
And red, blue, and every color beach chairs, and
Small yellow and blue boats brilliant
Against the pure, white, sugary strand.
Seagulls too enjoy the fray, flying quickly
Up and down and back and
Forth in play or search for food.
I think I'll take a little rest.

<u>*Spring Kiss*</u>

These poems were written at Destin Beach, Florida, while watching the sea from the balcony.

<u>*Spring Kiss*</u>

Spring, arriving, slowly, fast
In pastel shades of pink and green.
The sun with light winds shines sweetly down
To kiss the earth with full, warm, soft lips
To signal spring's beginning.

<u>The Color of Sand</u>

It is always interesting to see the color of the sand change with the weather, the time of day, and even the location of the beach.

The Color of Sand

Sand is not always white.
It is not always tan.
Sometimes it is gray and sometimes brown.
It can be pink or orange or salmon color.
Often it is blue or gold or mauve.
But it is always wild and beautiful to see.
It changes color with the prints of man
And prints of birds of every size.
The sun and sea, sunrise and
Sunset make their mark.
The wind, as well, plays its part.
So every moment you look upon the sand,
It is different every time.
Ever changing, every single instant
An interminable fascination:
Hypnotizing, mesmerizing,
And never ending.

Beach Umbrella Shade

At any time during a sunny day on the beach it is wonderful to be able to relax on a chair under an umbrella to enjoy the breeze and listen to the sea.

Beach Umbrella Shade

While now in quiet comfort
In umbrella shade, wrapped
Around by sun and sand and
Incessant sound of waves,
Transparent turquoise surf
Laps slowly onto shore,
Inviting all to join the din
Of people jumping and
Swimming in the sea.
So many people all around,
And still so silent, but for the
Sound of wind and ocean's pound.
Even amidst so much activity,
The greatness and the immensity
Of ocean, lends peace and
Calm tranquility.
It is said such pleasure
Is given only to sultans.

The Beach Clam

Often when you relax on the beach under an umbrella, circumstances make it necessary to arrange the umbrella and chair close together, creating a clam-like effect for the one sitting in the chair. It is a very pleasant experience.

The Beach Clam

Peering from beneath umbrella shade,
Warmed by sand below and
Cooled by breeze above,
Transfixed by gentle lapping
Of recurring waves, the
World seems luminous as a pearl.
Transparent air; transparent sea
Kept within a shelter none can see,
Perceiving nothing but light
Shimmering everywhere and through,
The hushing sounds of ocean all about.

Sing a Song of Orion

Orion was a 30 foot Morgan sailboat docked in Charleston, South Carolina. She sailed in Charleston Harbor and sometimes out in the ocean, south, to Beaufort, S.C. and other overnight anchorages north and south.

She sailed for a one month trip to the Bahamas motoring down the inland waterway to Ft. Lauderdale then sailing across to West End, Bahamas.

When leaving the Bahamas, she navigated three day s on the open ocean returning safely to the harbor at Charleston, making the first sight of land at the Edisto River 12 mile sea buoy light south of Charleston.

Sing a Song of Orion

She carried us through wind and rain,
Down waterways and back again,
Across the ocean inky blue,
To other places bright and new.
Through sunshine, wind, and stormy seas,
She ran before the slightest breeze.
She always floated light and fair,
To cut the water, wind, and air.
She is a beauty, proud and free,
A sailboat to the nth degree.
Sail on bright boat, sail on with zest
To all safe harbors come to rest.

The Last Sail

The Orion had to be sold. This poem is about her bittersweet, last cruise.

The Last Sail

The wind it blew, the sun it shone,
We sailed together, yet alone.
We sailed and sailed and tacked and jibed,
Before the wind we seemed to glide.
The sails close hauled brought us to heel,
We trimmed Orion most to keel.
She is as she will always be,
A very sailing symphony.
Our last sail was not her last,
But our last sail was free and fast!

<u>*Seven Young Maids from Romania*</u>

Sailing on board the Norwegian Cruise ship the Crown, on a
cruise to New England, the dining room servers were part of a
group
of very charming young Romanian women and men.

Seven Young Maids from Romania Sailing Aboard the Cruise Ship the Crown

Seven young maids from Romania
Sailed to sea on a cruising ship.
They sailed on a ship from Moravia
That had a royal relationship.

Seven young girls of Transylvania,
Dreaming of adventure and treasure,
Found life upon the restless sea
To be rather more work than was leisure.
At times the sea was very rough

And sometimes very calm,
The weather mostly fine but often foul,
Though their ship, that noble vessel,
Appeared to glide on the waves like a CROWN.

Effortlessly, the Crown, she seemed
To slip from port to shining port:
Sunrise into sunset and even on beyond,
And on again at sunrise, and on and on and on.

The ship sailed east and it sailed west,
And north and south besides:
'Neath golden skies and gray skies,
Through even swells and tides.

From city to fair city gate,
Smiling lips and sparkling eyes,
These seven young maids from Romania
Withstood their test of fate.

Too soon it seemed, the cruise dissolved,
In time too brief to measure:
For seven young maids from Romania,
Adventure was the treasure.

Ocean Speak

This poem was inspired by the sound of the sea while standing on the cabin balcony close to the ocean on a quiet, but breezy sunny day. Kathy may recognize this scene.

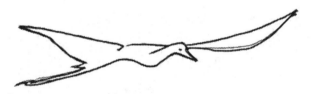

<u>Ocean Speak</u>

Watching the mighty ocean moving
By the railing on a sunny afternoon,
After days of cold and rainy weather.
The sharp bow of the big ship plows
Through calm and sparkling waters.
Calm but crested with white foam.
The sea speaks low to whisper
Unfathomable ocean secrets
On a soft and breathy, sunny breeze,
Trying to impart the ultimate and
Most silent secrets of the deep.
Wanting desperately to be understood,
But knowing the sweet and subtle
Language of the sea is just beyond
The listener's understanding.
It seems only a sweet seduction
Of sun and air and soft swishing
Sounds of waves against the bow.
It is a low, harmonic, gentle sound:
Singing like a soft and soothing siren's call.
Welcome is a bright, seductive day at sea.
And the secrets of the ocean,
Its secrets still remain.

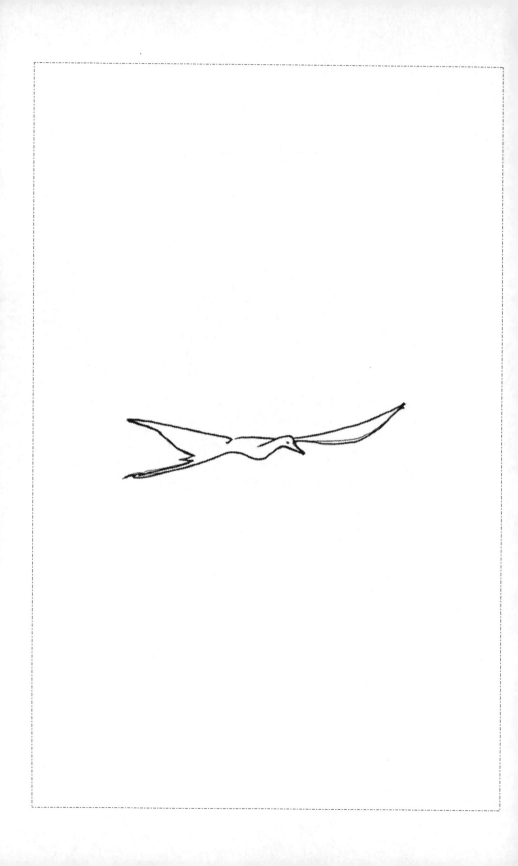

TWELVE KISSES

This set of poems describes just one day of each of the twelve months of the year.

January Kiss

In January mighty blizzards blow
That cover all the land with snow.
By day the snow is bright and clean
The light is frightful bright and clear.
Blue shadows on the snow appear
Cold-warm lavender, still and chill.
The air is cold and crisp and keen,
But in the bright and streaming light,
A hint of spring is seen.

February Kiss

The morning sun it shone
Straight down on me.
So gently and so tenderly,
The breeze it turned to kiss my cheek.
It spun light, fresh air to honey.
Always sweet and unexpected
In the momentary sweetness of sunlight
Sitting softly warm upon the eyes.
It is a gift, I know, and so short-lived.
It is a secret kiss from February,
Only, and especially, for me.

<u>*March Kiss*</u>

Sometimes in Virginia, there is a day so fine
When sun is warm but not too warm,
When wind, too, is warm and soft and just beyond a breeze
And wraps your skin in air so soft you feel as velvet as the air you
breathe.
It whirls your hair around your face with playful ease.
The day goes easy in its pass.
Like flights of yellow finches in the trees,
The sun shines brightly on green grass.
The wind continues with its tease.

April Kiss

The Happy Bluebirds

Flashing blue-colored wings in the sun,
The bluebirds live their busy, flitting
Lives, unaware the happiness they
Bring, just by being what they are.
A little bit of blue joy on the wing
To make the moment more serene.

May Kiss

The beautiful and gentle rose
Sways softly in the tender breeze.
A gift for the senses: sights,
Smells, and silence please.
Bluebirds and hummingbirds
Appear on the scene; they
Quickly appear and as quickly leave.
Remember deeply to savor it all.
For in a brief moment, it will be fall.

June Kiss

Birthday Kiss

Is this YOUR birthday today?
Nothing but sunshine like diamonds
Shining on the river.
Nothing but a gentle and cool breeze
In shade of large oak trees,
Nothing but warm sun and a cup of
Morning coffee, with a touch of chocolate,
Cards and gifts and chocolate birthday cake,
And friends galore surrounding you this day,
And wine and song and laughter.
A great gift is this day,
A beautiful and perfect gift.

July Kiss

Summer Day Experience

Soft breeze on warm and puffy air;
Bluebird sitting on its favorite perch
Flits there and here and back again,
Blue wings aflutter, resumes its search.
As with me, happiness is his this day.
No sound but wind; no thoughts or will,
To rise for anything requiring skill
Or thought of anything but being still.
Well, maybe read a book, but that distracts
From peace with nature and the wind.
The cool and peaceful scented breeze
Brings a whiff of earth and trees.
Silently, alone upon the chair,
Watch the shadows on the ground
And wonder what the bluebird found.

August Kiss

Sometimes in August there are beautiful days
That defy all predictions the weatherman says;
This is one of those mystical, magical days
That transforms itself gently into a bright haze.
High above everything as the wind twirls,
High in a bubble of shade and of breeze,
Sharing life only with birds and with
Leaves.
Surrounded by silence, by wind in the
Trees,
By breakfast and roses and books to
Read.
High cotton-white clouds set on deepest
Blue skies.
Beneath a whispering canopy of trees,
Time to enjoy a moment of ease.

September Kiss

End of Season

It's sad to take the garden down,
To see it turn from green to brown.
It dies so slowly, that is true,
From natures every color's hue
That in late summer seems
Most bright and strong,
Turning imperceptibly to mauves,
As winter takes its cue.

October Kiss

Secret Sounds of Fall

It is fresh tonight after rain,
So cool and, almost, but not cold,
But fresh and silent and empty
As in a long and almost lost refrain.
It is not dark but almost night,
And fall is silent with no starlight.
But sounds of fall are silent sounds,
And hollow are the sounds of fall,
And hollow are the sounds of night,
As fall descends so soft and light.

November Kiss

Only one day promised,
One last, warm day,
Embracing breeze, sunshine on an ocean
Of transparent, mellow yellow and
Bright, orange-colored trees.
Leaves like small stars suspended
Upon deepest, darkest, softest,
Mysterious moss green.
The late noon sun lights up the amber trees.
It dissipates: dissolving into sunlit,
Warm moist air, creating a transparent tapestry
Of muted gold, russets and lime greens.
Only one day promised, one last warm day,
Before the season's end,
Before the cold and rain and snow begin.

December Kiss

The air is moist and clear
And cool and fresh;
The sky is overcast,
The clouds hang low.
But still it is a lovely day,
So crisp and chill and new
And oh,
The soft and silent
Kiss of snow.

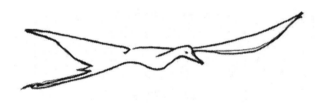

OTHER POEMS

The Amtrak Train Ride Home

This poem was inspired by a spectacular sunset observed when riding south on the Amtrak train from New York City in late December.

The Amtrak Train Ride Home

Distantly close, silently, slowly and quickly,
The sun exploded red and set down like a fireball into the earth,
Sending out fingers of red fire with smoky black tips.
Gently it continued the slow and inexorable
Descent to earth,
Altering colors to soft shades of rose,
And fading, reluctantly, at dusk,
Into rose-tinted,
Blackened, fingertips of gray.

White

In the month of January 2009, there was a not-unusual big
snowstorm in Washington, D.C.
At night, everything was dark, silent, and frozen—except for the
green and red traffic lights and a few streetlights reflecting on the
snow.

<u>White</u>

Looking through the window,
The night is flat and white with fallen snow,
And still and cold and oh so flat.
It is silent and oh so cold
And black and flat and frozen.
Mesmerized and quiet,
I stand frozen as the scene,
Unable to move or to look away from
The unreal, frigid emptiness outside.
But here and there is a little shine
That reflects the light
Of calm, white, frozen snow.
Falling backwards into flat,
Black, frozen night.

<u>Ode to Autumn</u>

In late August the weather changes only slightly, but enough to notice the season begins to change. The pleasures of warm weather must soon be gone. For some it is not a pleasant thought.

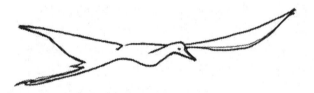

Ode to Autumn

It's sad to watch the summer die,
Take down the fountain with a sigh,
Pick the last roses, see the sun close,
Cool and long as earth begins to doze.

It's hard to know what's coming:
Cold weather, rain, and maybe snow.
And now you must wear a sweater,
For cool or cold or windy weather.

Too cool to sit beneath the trees,
Drink pink lemonade, enjoy the breeze.
It's hard to think that summer's over,
Much time and leisure lost forever.

How can you make the summer stay?
You cannot, and that fact's been laid.
Remember summer and its comforts;
Look to winter unafraid.

Remember South Carolina

In Myrtle Beach, South Carolina, in early December it is still warm enough to enjoy the beach. It is a good place to extend the summer.

Remember South Carolina

Remember South Carolina.
When other states are cold and dark,
The sun still shines warm in Myrtle Beach.
Time washed away by sun and by surf,
By delicate breezes and salt on the wind.
Blinded by sunlight, breathe in with
Closed eyes.
Hear rhythmical surf as it roils and sighs.
Sit for a while in a chair in the shade.
Stroll on soft sand as far as the pier.
Search for a starfish or tooth of a shark.
Watch the moon rise on the beach after dark.

The Chosen Rose

Selecting roses from the garden for the house is a great pleasure. The gardener learns which roses to pick for color and fragrance, and which last longest in a vase.

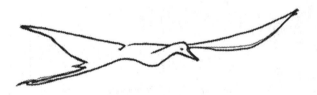

The Chosen Rose

All the beautiful roses,
In the kitchen they surround,
Pink, white, orange, and mauve.
All day long the gardener picked them
One by one
And put them in water in vases.
Not just any vases, but special vases,
Especially for each according to color,
Length of stem, and other
Important considerations.
Not every garden rose is chosen,
Many roses too far open, or far too dry.
They must be left to live and die.
But chosen ones come in the house
To open up and sing their fragrant song.
The gardener looks up and turns around,
Surprised by the sudden sound of song,
And unexpected multitude of beauty.

Forest Perfume

Sometimes, even in the city, there may be a patch of woods along a walk. Being still, it is possible to be surrounded by silence and the lovely fragrance of trees.

Forest Perfume

Stopping early evening near the woods,
The trees send down a lovely
Cloud of long-forgotten scent.
From earlier times remembered,
When did woods and trees abound,
Sending their perfume all around.

Fireflies

Fireflies arrive in June in Virginia. They begin to come out slowly as the sun sets. They are entertaining to watch.

Fireflies

Remembering many years before
Sweet cooling breezes in the
Summers evening silence,
And fireflies.
In early evening, while
Still visible green lawn,
Turns unhurriedly
To gold in lowering sun.
Seemingly from nowhere,
Small sparkling lights
Make their slow appearance.
Arising low from tips of grass.
Winking randomly and often,
They float quickly up in wildly
Blinking masses,
Into the darkening sky.
Against the dark trees' silhouette,
The Fireflies create a crescendo
Of winking lights.
They blink and blink and blink
And blink until,
As sky turns light in early dawn,
They disappear into the meadow
The way they came,
Waiting for the dark to come again.

<u>*Doing Nothing*</u>

These thoughts are written for those who are under stress and should learn that to relax is not as difficult as it seems.

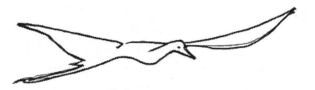

<u>Doing Nothing</u>

Doing nothing is quite an art
And can prove difficult at times.
But on a gentle day of breezes
From the mountain, the ocean,
Off the river, or just anywhere,
It is a place to start.
Turn off anything that makes a sound,
Except the sound of birds and wind.
Lean back, relax, put up your feet,
And empty out your thoughts.
Perhaps you will just fall asleep.
Perhaps your mind will find a way
To solve the knotty problems of the day,
Work out an old idea, or
Create something new.
All things, it seems, work out best
When there is nothing
Much to do.

<u>The Line</u>

Drawing and doodling is fun and can become a habit. It is surprising what can be the end result of a simple line drawing.

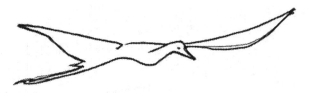

The Line

The line is made with ink and pen
It makes a circle now and then.
It is flirtatious and curvaceous,
Sometimes thick and
Sometimes thin.
Whatever you imagine,
Lines can be.
Lines can be straight,
They can be round:
They can be short or long.
They can go sideways or stand tall
Or even at a slant or
Opposite each other.
Think of something in your mind,
Take up a writing instrument.
Set it down on paper
Or just wave it in the air.
If you set it down on paper
You can see the line you make.
It often doesn't matter what it is,
There are no rules to making lines
So there can be no mistake,
Just let the pen describe
Your thoughts and maybe
In a moment your eyes
Will be surprised at
The lovely lines you've made.

<u>But Of Course—How Would It Be</u> <u>Otherwise?</u>

There are times a person does a small kindness that is not realized until later, when it is too late for thanks. However, it is possible kindness can be its own reward.

<u>But Of Course—How Would It Be Otherwise?</u>

Kindness given without thought
Is true kindness without plan
Or hope of reward.
It is often, by the recipient,
Gone unnoticed or realized too late for
Thanks,
But true kindness is a gift for giver and
Receiver both.
Noticed or unnoticed, it is a gentle side
To the universe, benefiting all.
The more kindness, the more benefit.

<u>*Wise Words*</u>

This poem was written because of a true experience had by the author when landscaping the hill in the rear garden of her residence.

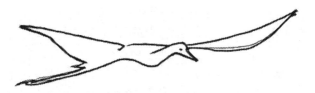

<u>Wise Words</u>

When rumbling down the hill that day
In a truck too big for me
I struggled looking right and left
To obtain a way to see.

The hill was lumpy, bumpy, muddy.
It made the big truck rock and lean.
I was afraid that all at once
The truck would soon careen.

Steep was the hill and rutty too.
I was down too far for flight.
No matter that the sky was blue,
It caused me quite a fright.

So halfway down I warned my friend.
There's danger down the hill,
'Cause I was pointed downward,
Convinced that I would spill.

My friend smiled and three words said
That calmed me on that day.
I ever afterward remembered them
When trouble came my way.

The words he said, with laughing eyes,
Seemed so simple and so clear,
I thought that day and after,
Why did I ever fear?

And now I guess you wonder
What words caused my heart to cheer,
To clear my head and make me smile
And take away my fear.

Three words there were, and only three,
Spoken quietly from him to me.
NEVER DOUBT YOURSELF,
He said. He said it only once.

Three words he said, and only three,
And maybe soon forgot.
How would he know how oft-recalled
When in a fearsome spot.
NEVER DOUBT YOURSELF!
A clear and easy thought.
When I've said them to myself again,
My fears have come to naught.

So I can smile and say to THEM,
THEM frightened by the fray,
NEVER DOUBLE YOURSELF;
Your fears will go away.

Even if the fears are real,
They can by you be dispelled.
Take an easy breath and smile.
Your fears will go your way.

NEVER DOUBT YOURSELF,
A quiet man once said.
Changing my life and the many
To whom the word was spread.

And so I say to you, dear friend,
Go effortlessly through life,
But when fear does come your way,
<u>NEVER DOUBT YOURSELF</u>.

<u>There Goes My Hawk</u>

Often in the city, or in other unexpected places and at unexpected times, hawks, eagles, raptors, and other large birds can be sighted in the sky, near or far away.

The hawk in the poem is real and always exciting to observe.

There Goes My Hawk

There he flies so swiftly by,
Very difficult to see.
On silent wings he dashes
From one sky to another.
He causes such excitement
In his swiftness, grace,
And beauty
But does not linger one place
Long enough
To gauge his shape or color.
Suddenly he ups and flies
From one tree to another.
He is a small hawk   from his size
Probably a "she."
The hawk that usually plies these
Skies is probably her brother.
No, my hawk is a larger bird,
There's no relation there.
He is larger and not so quick
And has great wings to flare.
Sometimes he finds a place to perch
Upon the largest tree.
He sits there for the longest

Time and doesn't move a muscle,
And if the crows don't see him,
With quick and hawkish eye
He'll spy beneath
A lunch or dinner's tussle.
A beautiful, amazing bird, and
Wonderful to see.
So silent and so calm
Upon his favorite tree.
If he would just sit closer,
So his markings could be seen,
Identified by color
So we could know his name.
Someday this large, proud bird
May be close enough to see
And judge by size and markings
By what to shout his name.
But until then we'll just jump up
When we see him fly
And say, "There goes my hawk,"
And that will be just fine.

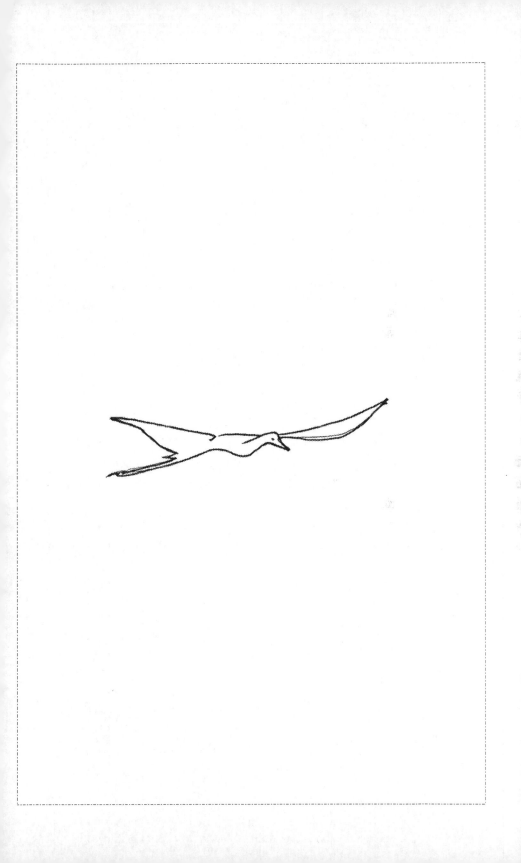

<u>Dottie "Sez"</u>

Dottie was a friend who joined us on some of our travels. She was very sweet, full of fun and sage sayings from her home in North Carolina. She was a proud Tar Heel.

Dottie "Sez"

If you're feeling low and you'd like to know
The road to a happier way,
Drive along with Dottie
And hear her exclaim,
"Oh, What a Beautiful Day!"

Seeing atop a distant hill
A picturesque estate.
How wonderful must it be
To experience
This quiet, idyllic spot.
"Self-sufficiency is required out here,"
Did quietly Dottie say.

Just think of the view
And the vast green expanse
To admire as you go

You must admit,
Did Dottie say,
"That's a lot of grass to mow."

With all the views so gorgeous,
As well as a wonderful setting,
One must enjoy this lovely park.
"It is too far from the grocery,"
Was Dottie's wise remark.

Well, it's all a lot to think about,
Going along the way,
Still all things considered,
Like Dottie says,
"What a Beautiful Day!"

STAR SPANGLED

Patriotic Poems

Present History Remembered

Yes, it was there, the world to see.
So appealingly and excitingly different,
With much to learn from it.
Having seen and absorbed it all,
Returning home was all the sweeter.
To see, once again, the openness
And freedom of the skies and the land of home.
Freedom seen in the arch of the full moon,
Soaring in a clear sky high above the trees or
In the evening skies of pale turquoise
Laced in pink and mauve against
Dark green evening silhouettes.
Are they remembered, those who
Lived early in our history?
Who designed, unwittingly, but with
Great affection, much care and
Inspiration, our future as a nation.
As a nation, do we think and speak
With the humanity and purposeful
Thought as planned by those who went before?
Or have we lost the thread of integrity inspired
By those who wrought our great beginnings.
We must continue, if we love our land and freedom,
To look at history and study the wisdom
Of those who went before.
They who planned so exceptionally well
For the future of our beloved land.

Joy, Hallelujah and the Fourth of July

Sing for joy: Hosannas and Hallelujahs.
The Fourth of July is here again.
Raise the flags,
Set out bunting of red, white, and blue.
Bring forth the food,
Set off fireworks.
Sing Hallelujahs for our freedom,
Sing for the blessings of
Our people and our country.

Fourth of July is here again!!!

Bunting is for joy,
Food for singing Hallelujahs.
Once again the celebration comes.
Tentative smiles greet festive beginnings.
And now smile wide and sing out
Hosannas for joy and celebration
For the Blessings of our special Land.

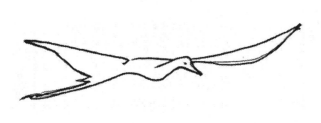

POEMS ABOUT TIME

Sunshine and Fairy Dust

Sunshine and fairy dust,
The inside of a forest,

Sun and shade,
Reflections in a pool.
Love?
Or maybe you already
Know these things don't last forever.

Sunshine and fairy dust,
Reflections in a pool,
Sun and shade,
The inside of a forest,
All things ephemeral?
The heart of eternity.

Sunshine and Fairy Dust

Sunshine and fairy dust,
The inside of a forest,

Sun and shade,
Reflections in a pool.
Love?
Or maybe you already
Know these things do last forever.

Sunshine and fairy dust,
Reflections in a pool,
Sun and shade,
The inside of a forest,
All things ephemeral?
The heart of eternity.

<u>*Endings*</u>

This poem was written while watching the final Oprah Winfrey
TV show. The thought of the show ending was very sad. It was a
reminder of the last Tonight Show with Johnny Carson, and the
death of Liz Taylor. They were famous people who were part of
everyday life for many years. They were never supposed to go
away.

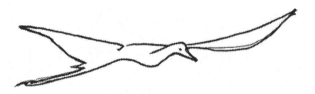

Endings

Endings are sweet,
They make you cry.
After years believing in forever,
In times unchanging,
Believing in the constancy of life,
Softly or with surprise,
The END arrives,
Life changed forever after.
Endings are not the END.
The END continues in mind and heart
As memories smile at times remembered.
How good to have been there,
To have experienced the sweet and gentle
END.

This Moment

This moment is present time,
It is happy, sad, brilliant, or dull,
Or as many things other as there can be.
At this moment I am beautiful;
My long dress sparkles in the spotlight.
My voice is lovely, trilling high to low
And back again,
Pleasing the audience, I can see.
My one perfect moment IS NOW,
And many more such moments I wish there to be.
A brilliant performance here and gone.
But here am I, my goal achieved,
What the future holds is yet to be
This magic moment has disappeared.
It lives only
Forever in memory.

Time Unseen

Steps in life and unremembered time surround us all.
Thoughts constant and instantly forgotten,
Movements made and lost for all time.
Why remember every moment when
Life, perhaps, will be long?
One invisible step blends into another.
Lost forever in UNSEEN TIME.
Time is lost without our knowledge.
It cannot be watched as it goes by,
Only possibly by watching a moment of
Time passing in surrounding lives,
Or in imagined memory of past events.
Steps taken down will not go back up in time.
A moment of laughter in the sun
Is gone but for its memory.
A lovely kiss is over at its ending
But only in imagined sights
And sounds remembered.
Each moment of our lives lasts forever or
Disappears UNSEEN into amorphous TIME.
It will not be visible as it disappears.

<u>The Last Hoorah!</u>

The last hoorah begins unknowingly.
It proceeds forward into time without concern.
It goes curiously step by step
Into the blank unknown,
Full of hope and wonder for future time.
And so it continues from moment to moment,
Greeting strange and wondrous events
With so much grace and courage,
And cannot see the end until it comes close by.
Looking backward,
Knowing the end is somehow near,
But at an undetermined time,
The best exit possible can be planned and executed.
Perhaps it will be the next-to-the
LAST HOORAH;
And so on.

Once In A Lifetime

I have been before to the orange mountain,
Sniffed the evening breeze at orange sunset,
Watched the sun sink slowly down the back of earth.
It was beautiful to see and feel,
Definitely worth the climb;
An experience to treasure through the years.
But there are other colored mountains to be seen,
Felt, experienced and enjoyed.
The green and the purple mountain
And other colored mountains
Wait and are still to be climbed.
Each one more, or just as lovely, as the last,
And all it takes is time.
So the orange mountain I will not see again,
But am comforted by the memory
Of the orange mountain that remains.

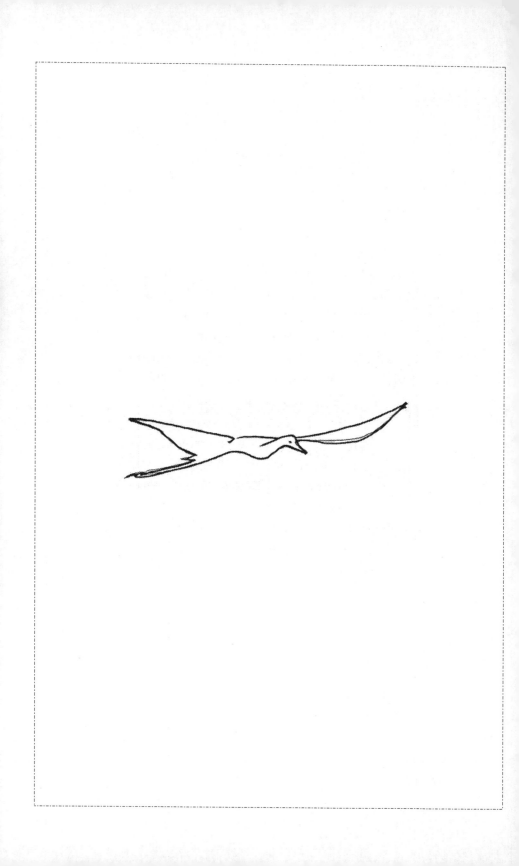

ABOUT THE AUTHOR

E.M. Adams was born in June 1941 in Portsmouth, Virginia, and moved at age five to Hilton Village in Newport News, Virginia. She attended the historic old Hilton Village Elementary School, located right upon the James River. The school playground and its pier were part of growing up in the Tidewater area amidst all the beautiful rivers and waterways of the region. It was a sunny, charming, peaceful place to spend early years. Boating and being on the water were a part of everyone's existence in the tidewater area, so water, weather, wind and tides, rain and storm, fishing and crabbing, and more became second nature to the residents of this part of Virginia.

Her adult career began as a young summer employee working as a secretary for the Officers' Training School at Fort Eustis, Virginia. After this experience, she studied business at James Madison University (previously Madison College) and then changed schools to study art at Virginia Commonwealth University (previously Richmond Professional Institute). She graduated from there with a BFA.

After graduation she began a career as art teacher which lasted fifteen years until she began a second career in real estate. Now she begins a new occupation in writing.

Elizabeth L. Meissner married Andrew J. Adams, Jr., an officer in the USAF, in 1967 and after wonderful assignments and many lovely travels will soon celebrate forty-five years of marriage.